RITE I

A EUCHARISTIC MANUAL
FOR CHILDREN

Eileen Garrison
and
Gayle Albanese

Morehouse Publishing
NEW YORK · HARRISBURG · DENVER

Morehouse Publishing
A division of Church Publishing Incorporated

ISBN 978-0-8192-1343-3

Library of Congress Catalog Card Number 84-60217

Printed in the United States of America

This book is dedicated to all children,
to open their minds and hearts
to spiritual growth and communication with God.

"Let the children come to me and do not
stop them, because the Kingdom of God
belongs to such as these."

—Matthew 19:14

Adaptation and Composition

Eileen Garrison

Artistic Concept

Gayle Albanese

Cover Art and Illustrations

Charles Dickinson

Special Appreciation to

The Rev. Richard E. Lundberg
Rector of St. Simon's Episcopal Church
Arlington Heights, Illinois 60005

and

The Rev. John Throop
Curate of St. Simon's Episcopal Church (1981-83)

for assistance in editing

and

The Stratford Publisher, Ltd.

for assistance in publication

This book belongs to _____

THIS BOOKLET was designed to help the young child learn to participate in the Liturgy. It is a tool to encourage responding, praying, and singing at appropriate times. Parents can help by locating hymns in the Hymnal, indicating corresponding sections in *The Book of Common Prayer,* and by helping the child follow some of the longer prayers, such as the Gloria and the Creed, which have been omitted in this simplified text. It is hoped that *The Book of Common Prayer* will be used for total participation as the child's interest and ability permit.

HOW TO USE THIS BOOK

You will see little pictures that will help you know what to do while you pray. This is what they mean:

 STAND UP   SIT DOWN   KNEEL

When you see a box around the words, pay special attention.

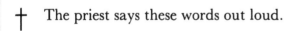
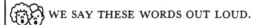

† The priest says these words out loud.

WE SAY THESE WORDS OUT LOUD.

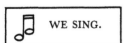 WE SING.

Ask an adult to help you find the right hymn in the big book of songs called the Hymnal.

crucifer   torch bearers   choir

acolytes   layreaders   assisting priest   celebrant

PROCESSIONAL

 The priest, acolytes and choir come into the church.

 Look in the Hymnal.

---

† Blessed be God: Father, Son, and Holy Spirit.

AND BLESSED BE HIS KINGDOM, NOW AND FOREVER. AMEN.

Say or Sing:

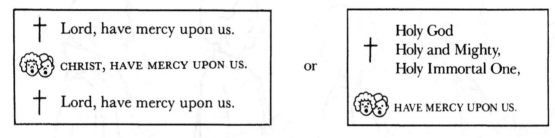

† Lord, have mercy upon us.

CHRIST, HAVE MERCY UPON US.

† Lord, have mercy upon us.

or

Holy God
† Holy and Mighty,
Holy Immortal One,

HAVE MERCY UPON US.

or, sometimes we pray or sing:

† Glory be to God on high.

This prayer is to praise, bless, worship, glorify, and give thanks to God.

GATHER
IN THE
LORD'S
NAME

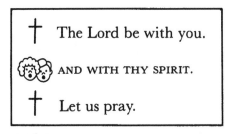

† The Lord be with you.

 AND WITH THY SPIRIT.

† Let us pray.

COLLECT  or

The priest says a prayer with special thoughts for today. When it is over, we say:

 AMEN.

LESSONS

We listen to readings from the Bible.

The *first reading* comes from the Old Testament. This part of the Bible was written long before Jesus was born. We hear how God has spoken and worked through His people for thousands of years.

The *Psalm* is a hymn or poem of the people of Israel that Jesus used.

The *second reading* is usually part of a letter. It was written by a person who was alive when Jesus was on earth, or who knew about Jesus. This lesson reminds us how to be better Christians, or followers of Jesus Christ.

After each reading we say:

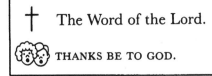

† The Word of the Lord.

THANKS BE TO GOD.

LISTEN
TO THE
WORD
OF GOD

GOSPEL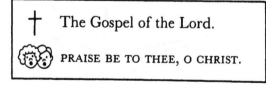

✝ The Holy Gospel of Our Lord Jesus Christ according to Matthew, Mark, Luke, or John.

GLORY BE TO THEE, O LORD.

LISTEN TO THE WORD OF GOD

Gospel means "good news." The good news is who Jesus is and what he did. Jesus teaches us to be more like him when we listen to the Gospel.

When the Gospel is over, we say:

✝ The Gospel of the Lord.

PRAISE BE TO THEE, O CHRIST.

SERMON

The priest talks to us about what the lessons and the Gospel mean.

CREED

We say out loud what Christians believe.

We believe in one God, Who made us and all things.

We believe in Jesus Christ, the only Son of God, who saves us.

We believe in the Holy Spirit, who helps us grow to be like Jesus Christ.

PROCLAIM
AND
RESPOND
TO THE
WORD
OF GOD

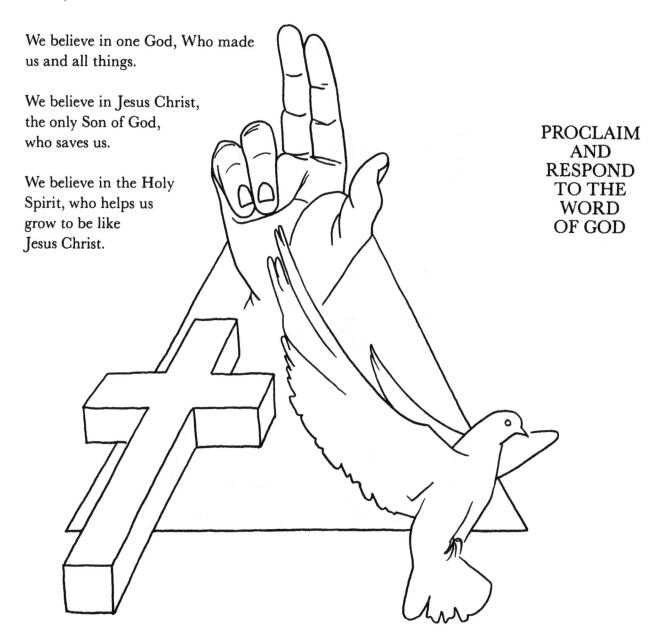

11

☩ Let us pray for the whole state of Christ's Church and the world.

PRAYERS OF THE PEOPLE or

We pray for our bishops and our priests, and all the people in our church.

We pray for all the leaders in the government.

PRAY
FOR THE
WORLD
AND THE
CHURCH

We pray for all the people who are sick, or sad, or in trouble.

We pray for the souls of all the people who have died.

We ask God to please hear our prayers,
for His Son Jesus Christ's sake.

12

CONFESSION

We tell God we are sorry for things we have done wrong. We are sorry, too, for things we should have done, but didn't do. We will try harder to love God and to follow Him.

ABSOLUTION

God loves us. He will certainly forgive us.

THE PEACE

> ✝ The peace of the Lord be always with you.
>
> AND WITH THY SPIRIT.

EXCHANGE
THE
PEACE

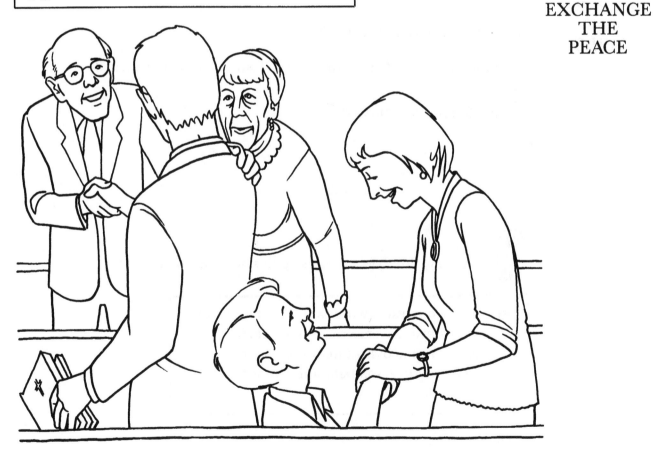

We shake hands or hug each other to wish God's peace to each other.

OFFERTORY

We offer ourselves to God. We give money to the church to help us do God's work, and to thank God for all His blessings.

PREPARE THE TABLE

The priest may wash his hands as he prays.

People carry our gifts of bread and wine and our gifts of money up to the altar.

All our gifts are offered to God.

 On many Sundays we will sing this or some other hymn:

> PRAISE GOD FROM WHOM ALL BLESSINGS FLOW.
> PRAISE HIM ALL CREATURES HERE BELOW.
> PRAISE HIM ABOVE YE HEAVENLY HOST.
> PRAISE FATHER, SON, AND HOLY GHOST.
> AMEN.

THE GREAT THANKSGIVING

✝ The Lord be with you.

AND WITH THY SPIRIT.

✝ Lift up your hearts.

WE LIFT THEM UP UNTO THE LORD.

✝ Let us give thanks to our Lord God.

IT IS MEET AND RIGHT SO TO DO.

**MAKE
THE
EUCHARIST**

♪ HOLY, HOLY, HOLY, LORD GOD OF HOSTS:
HEAVEN AND EARTH ARE FULL OF THY GLORY.
GLORY BE TO THEE, O LORD MOST HIGH.
BLESSED IS HE THAT COMETH IN THE NAME OF THE LORD.
HOSANNA IN THE HIGHEST.

THE GREAT THANKS-GIVING

 At the Last Supper, the night before Jesus died, he gave us a special gift.

Jesus took bread, gave thanks for it, broke it, and gave it to his disciples.

He said, "Take, eat, this is my Body."

Then, after supper, Jesus took wine.

He gave thanks for it, and said to his disciples,
"Drink ye all of this; for this is my Blood.

Do this in remembrance of me."

Today we offer bread and wine in the same way, just as Jesus told us to do.

The special gift is Jesus, himself.

He is with us in his special way in the Eucharist.

✝ By whom, and with whom, in the unity of the Holy Ghost, all honor and glory be unto thee, O Father Almighty, world without end.

AMEN.

✝ And now, as our Savior Christ has taught us, we are bold to say,

OUR FATHER, WHO ART IN HEAVEN,

HALLOWED BE THY NAME,

THY KINGDOM COME,

THY WILL BE DONE,

ON EARTH AS IT IS IN HEAVEN.

GIVE US THIS DAY OUR DAILY BREAD.

AND FORGIVE US OUR TRESPASSES,

AS WE FORGIVE THOSE WHO TRESPASS AGAINST US.

AND LEAD US NOT INTO TEMPTATION,

BUT DELIVER US FROM EVIL.

FOR THINE IS THE KINGDOM, AND THE POWER, AND THE GLORY,

FOR EVER AND EVER.

AMEN.

THE GREAT THANKS-GIVING

BREAKING OF THE BREAD

The priest breaks the Bread we have offered.

✝ Christ our Passover is sacrificed for us.

THEREFORE LET US KEEP THE FEAST.

This anthem or some other may be sung or said:

♪ O LAMB OF GOD, THAT TAKEST AWAY THE SINS OF THE WORLD, HAVE MERCY UPON US.

O LAMB OF GOD, THAT TAKEST AWAY THE SINS OF THE WORLD, HAVE MERCY UPON US.

O LAMB OF GOD, THAT TAKEST AWAY THE SINS OF THE WORLD, GRANT US THY PEACE.

✝ The Gifts of God for the People of God.

SHARE THE GIFTS OF GOD

The priest and people share the Bread and Wine
at the altar and recall Jesus with us today.

✝ Let us pray.

We thank God for Jesus' spiritual presence in the Eucharist. We ask God to
help us do His work.

✝ The Blessing of God Almighty, the Father, the Son, and the
Holy Spirit, be upon you and remain with you forever.

AMEN.

✝ Let us go forth in the name of Christ.

THANKS BE TO GOD.

The celebration of the Eucharist is over. We pray quietly to give our own thanks, and ask God's help to live as Christians all week long.

RECESSIONAL

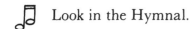 Look in the Hymnal.

The priest, acolytes and choir leave the altar.

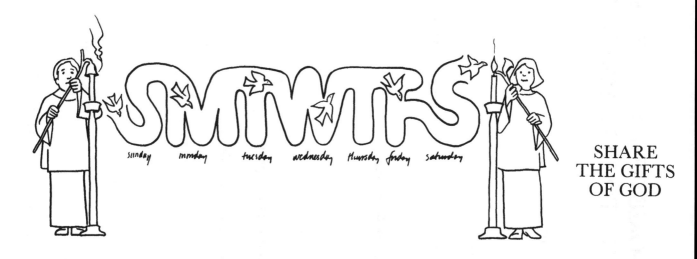

SHARE
THE GIFTS
OF GOD

HERE ARE SOME OF THE WORDS USED WITH DEFINITIONS TO HELP YOU UNDERSTAND

acolyte – a boy or girl who helps the priest.

almighty – having all power.

altar – the table where sacrifice is offered to God.

Amen – a word we use to say that we agree with what has been said. It means "This is the way it is" or "This is true."

Baptism – the rite by which we become Christians.

believe – to think something is true.

Bible – the book of writings inspired by God.

bless – to guard or protect; it can also mean to praise.

choir – people who serve the church through music.

Christians – followers of Jesus Christ and his teachings.

covenant –an agreement.

creed – a short statement of what we believe.

disciple – a person who is learning.

Eucharist – the sacrament which Jesus gave us to recall his life, death, and rising from the dead.

faith – trust in God.

hosanna – a word of praise to the Lord.

A

hymn — a prayer or poem that is sung.

meet — the right thing to do.

mercy — willingness to help or forgive.

New Testament — the part of the Bible that contains the story of Jesus' life and work and teachings about him.

Old Testament — the part of the Bible that tells about God's relationship with His people before Jesus was born.

Passover — the name of the annual Jewish feast day which recalls God's saving His people in Egypt.

praise — to say wonderful things.

pray — to speak to God.

priest — a person who serves God in a special way, especially by offering the Eucharist, representing Jesus, preaching the Gospel, and caring for the people of God.

processional — the movement of a group of persons into church which signals the beginning of the service. A hymn may be sung at this time.

proclaim — to say openly.

rite — a certain way to do something.

sacrament — a sign that tells about something we can't see.

spirit — the part of us that is like God.

symbol — something we can see that really stands for something else. The American flag is a symbol of the United States.

worship — the acts of paying honor to God, by praying, singing, kneeling, and taking part in the service.

B

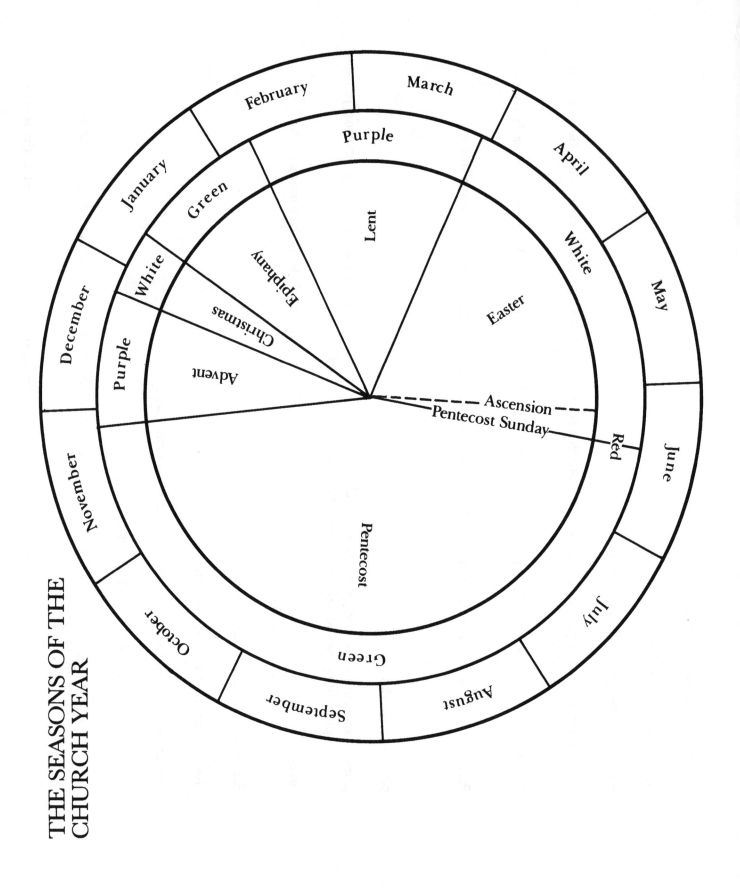

THE SEASONS OF THE
CHURCH YEAR

C

RITE II

A EUCHARISTIC MANUAL
FOR CHILDREN

Eileen Garrison
and
Gayle Albanese

Morehouse Publishing
NEW YORK · HARRISBURG · DENVER

Morehouse Publishing
A division of Church Publishing Incorporated

ISBN 978-0-8192-1343-3

Library of Congress Catalog Card Number 84-60217

Printed in the United States of America

This book is dedicated to all children,
to open their minds and hearts
to spiritual growth and communication with God.

"Let the children come to me and do not
stop them, because the Kingdom of God
belongs to such as these."

—Matthew 19:14

Adaptation and Composition

Eileen Garrison

Artistic Concept

Gayle Albanese

Cover Art and Illustrations

Charles Dickinson

Special Appreciation to

The Rev. Richard E. Lundberg
Rector of St. Simon's Episcopal Church
Arlington Heights, Illinois 60005

and

The Rev. John Throop
Curate of St. Simon's Episcopal Church (1981-83)

for assistance in editing

and

The Stratford Publisher, Ltd.

for assistance in publication

This book belongs to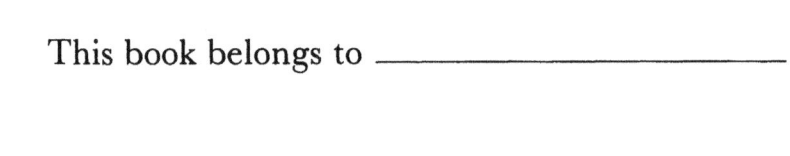

THIS BOOKLET was designed to help the young child learn to participate in the Liturgy. It is a tool to encourage responding, praying, and singing at appropriate times. Parents can help by locating hymns in the Hymnal, indicating corresponding sections in *The Book of Common Prayer,* and by helping the child follow some of the longer prayers, such as the Gloria and the Creed, which have been omitted in this simplified text. It is hoped that *The Book of Common Prayer* will be used for total participation as the child's interest and ability permit.

HOW TO USE THIS BOOK

You will see little pictures that will help you know what to do while you pray. This is what they mean:

STAND UP   SIT DOWN   KNEEL

When you see a box around the words, pay special attention.

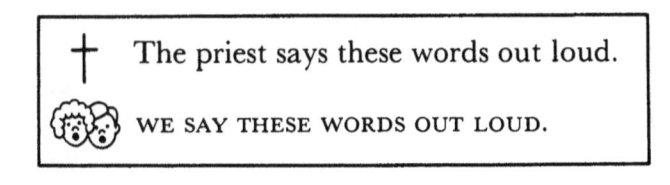

✝ The priest says these words out loud.

WE SAY THESE WORDS OUT LOUD.

♪ WE SING.

Ask an adult to help you find the right hymn in the big book of songs called the Hymnal.

crucifer   torch bearers   choir

acolytes   layreaders   assisting priest   celebrant

RITE II

GATHER
IN THE
LORD'S
NAME

PROCESSIONAL

The priest, acolytes and choir come into church.

♩ Look in the Hymnal.

✝ Blessed be God: Father, Son, and Holy Spirit.

 AND BLESSED BE HIS KINGDOM, NOW AND FOREVER. AMEN.

If there is a Baptism, we say this:

> ✝ There is one Body and one Spirit;
>
> 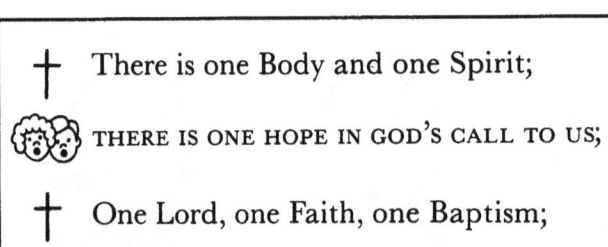 THERE IS ONE HOPE IN GOD'S CALL TO US;
>
> ✝ One Lord, one Faith, one Baptism;
>
> ONE GOD AND FATHER OF ALL.

Go to page 9.

GATHER IN THE LORD'S NAME

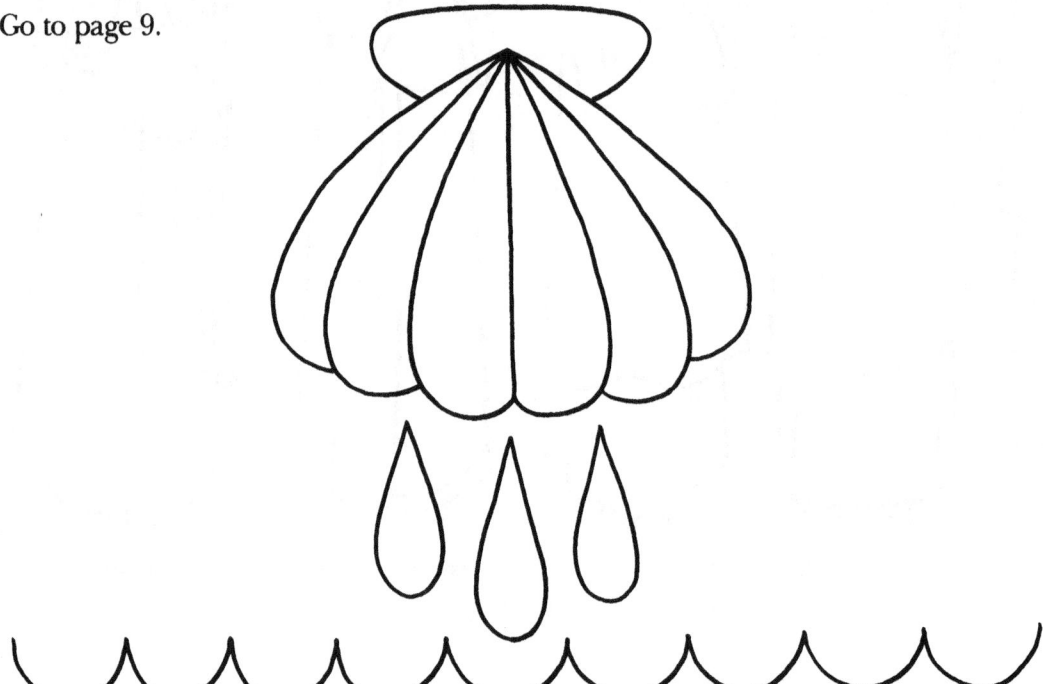

Say or sing:

> ✝ Lord have mercy.
>
> CHRIST HAVE MERCY.
>
> ✝ Lord have mercy.

or

> ✝ Holy God
> Holy and Mighty,
> Holy Immortal One,
>
> HAVE MERCY UPON US.

Sometimes we pray or sing:

✝ Glory to God in the highest, and peace to his people on earth.

This is a prayer of praise and thanksgiving.

> † The Lord be with you.
>
> 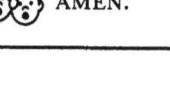 AND ALSO WITH YOU.
>
> † Let us pray.

COLLECT  or

The priest says a prayer with special thoughts for today. When it is over, we say:

> 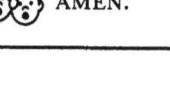 AMEN.

LESSONS

LISTEN TO THE WORD OF GOD

The *first reading* comes from the Old Testament. This part of the Bible was written long before Jesus was born. We hear how God has spoken and worked through His people for thousands of years.

The *Psalm* is a hymn or poem of the people of Israel that Jesus used.

The *second reading* is usually part of a letter. It was written by a person who was alive when Jesus was on earth, or who knew about Jesus. This lesson reminds us how to be better Christians, or followers of Jesus Christ.

After each reading we say:

> † The Word of the Lord.
>
> 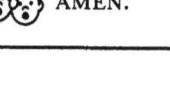 THANKS BE TO GOD.

GOSPEL

> ✝ The Holy Gospel of Our Lord Jesus Christ according to Matthew, Mark, Luke, or John.
>
> 👥 GLORY TO YOU, LORD CHRIST.

LISTEN TO THE WORD OF GOD

Gospel means "good news." The good news is who Jesus is and what he did. Jesus teaches us to be more like him when we listen to the Gospel.

When the Gospel is over, we say:

> ✝ The Gospel of the Lord.
>
> 👥 PRAISE TO YOU, LORD CHRIST.

SERMON

The priest talks to us about what the lessons and the Gospel mean.
If there is a Baptism, turn to page 12.

CREED

We say out loud what Christians believe.

We believe in one God, Who made
us and all things.

We believe in Jesus Christ,
the only Son of God,
who saves us.

We believe in the Holy
Spirit, who helps us
grow to be like
Jesus Christ.

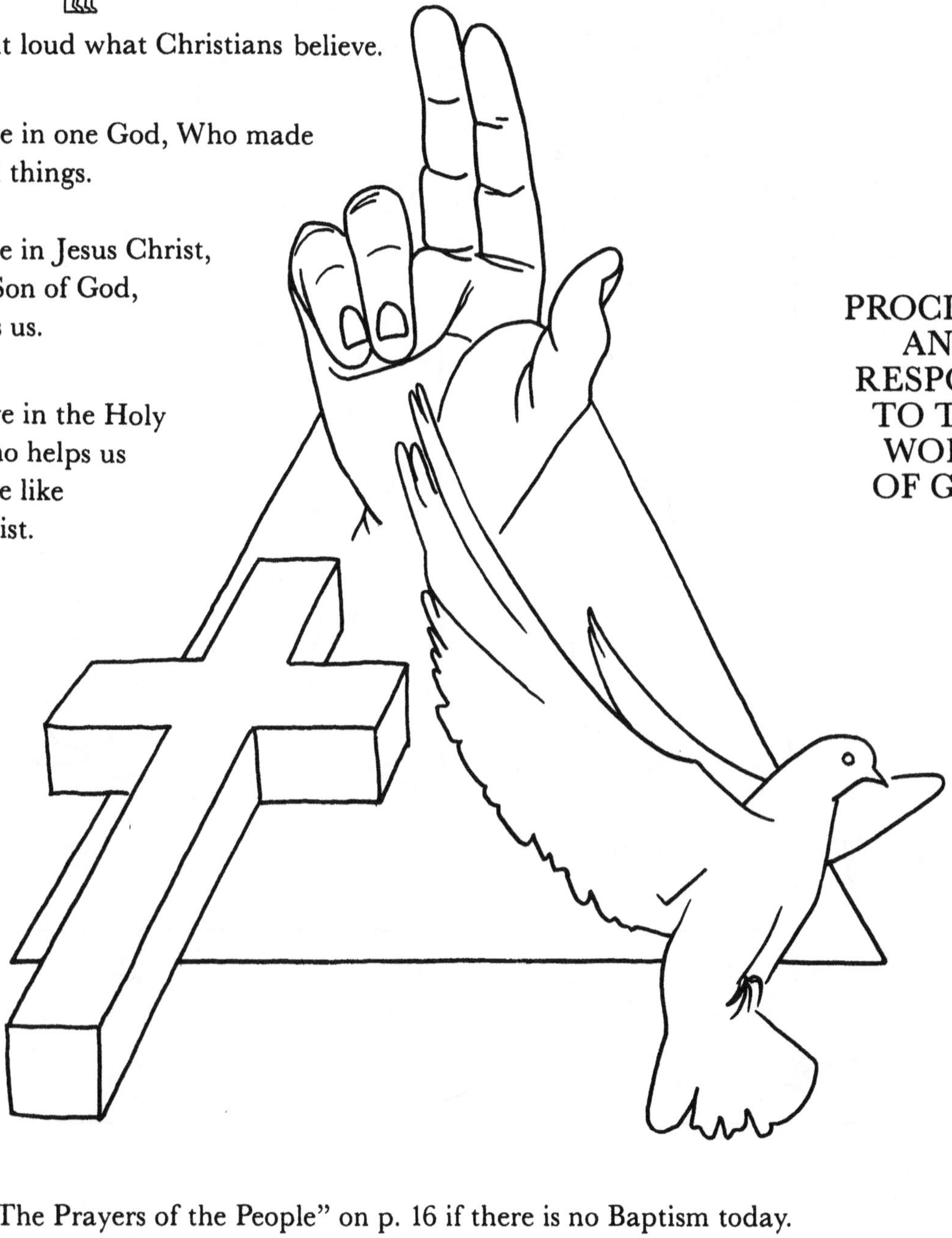

PROCLAIM
AND
RESPOND
TO THE
WORD
OF GOD

Turn to "The Prayers of the People" on p. 16 if there is no Baptism today.

The person to be baptized, the Godparents or Sponsors, and the members of the family join the priest at the front of the church.

HOLY BAPTISM

The priest asks all of us to help the person who is being baptized grow as a Christian.

✝ Will you who witness these vows do all in your power to support these persons in their life in Christ?

WE WILL.

We renew our own baptismal vows.

THE BAPTISMAL COVENANT

✝ Do you believe in God the Father?

I BELIEVE IN GOD, THE FATHER ALMIGHTY, CREATOR OF HEAVEN AND EARTH.

✝ Do you believe in Jesus Christ, the Son of God?

I BELIEVE IN JESUS CHRIST, HIS ONLY SON, OUR LORD

✝ Do you believe in God the Holy Spirit?

I BELIEVE IN THE HOLY SPIRIT.

✝ Will you continue in the apostles' teaching and fellowship, in the breaking of bread, and in the prayers?

I WILL, WITH GOD'S HELP.

✝ Will you persevere in resisting evil and whenever you fall into sin, repent and return to the Lord?

I WILL, WITH GOD'S HELP.

✝ Will you proclaim by word and example the Good News of God in Christ?

I WILL, WITH GOD'S HELP.

✝ Will you seek and serve Christ in all persons, loving your neighbor as yourself?

I WILL, WITH GOD'S HELP.

✝ Will you strive for justice and peace among all people, and respect the dignity of every human being?

I WILL, WITH GOD'S HELP.

We pray for the person to be baptized, and for ourselves.

✝ Deliver them, O Lord, from the way of sin and death.

LORD, HEAR OUR PRAYER.

✝ Open their hearts to your grace and truth.

LORD, HEAR OUR PRAYER.

✝ Fill them with your holy and life-giving Spirit.

LORD, HEAR OUR PRAYER.

✝ Keep them in the faith and communion of your holy Church.

LORD, HEAR OUR PRAYER.

✝ Teach them to love others in the power of the Spirit.

LORD, HEAR OUR PRAYER.

✝ Send them into the world in witness to your love.

LORD, HEAR OUR PRAYER.

✝ Bring them to the fullness of your peace and glory.

LORD, HEAR OUR PRAYER.

HOLY BAPTISM

The priest blesses the water.

✝ The Lord be with you.

AND ALSO WITH YOU.

✝ Let us give thanks to the Lord our God.

IT IS RIGHT TO GIVE HIM THANKS AND PRAISE.

The priest thanks God for the gift of water. Water is an important symbol in the Bible. Through the sacrament of Baptism, we share in Jesus' death and new life. When we are baptized, we are welcomed into the Christian Church.

THE BAPTISM

The priest pours water on the person to be baptized, while saying:

† (Name), I baptize you in the name of the Father, and of the Son, and of the Holy Spirit.

 AMEN.

† (Name), you are sealed by the Holy Spirit in Baptism and marked as Christ's own for ever.

 AMEN.

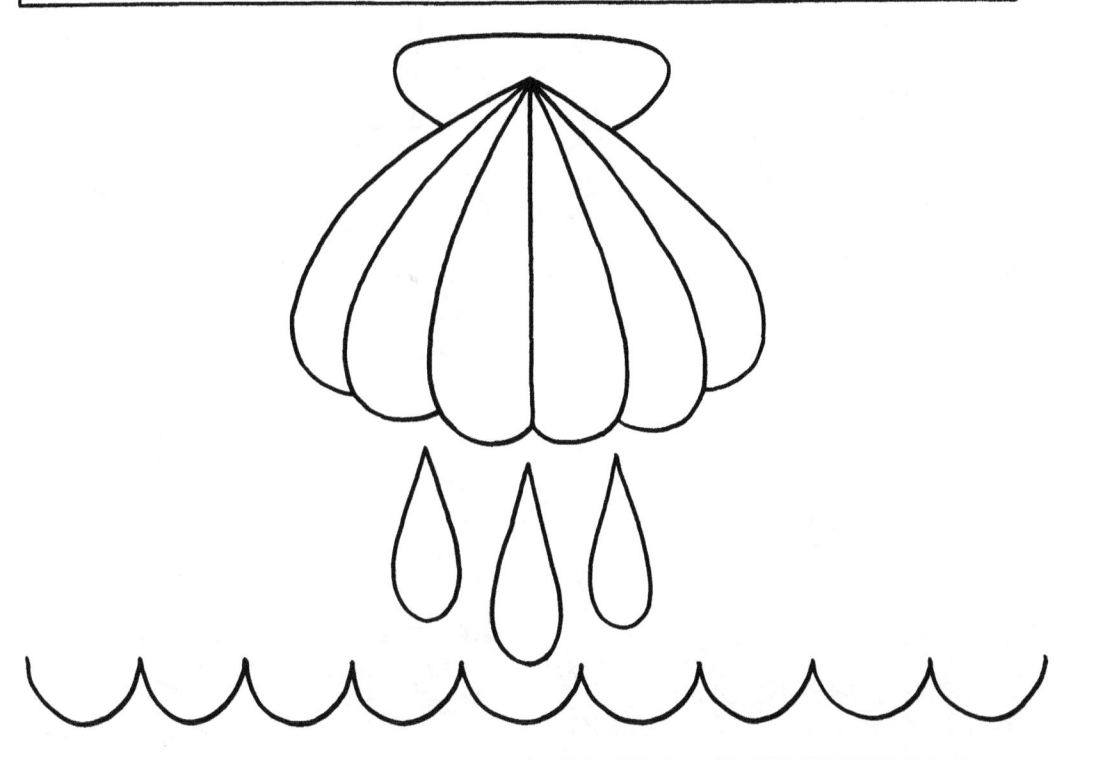

HOLY
BAPTISM

† Let us welcome the newly baptized.

 WE RECEIVE YOU INTO THE HOUSEHOLD OF GOD.

CONFESS THE FAITH OF CHRIST CRUCIFIED, PROCLAIM HIS RESURRECTION, AND SHARE WITH US IN HIS ETERNAL PRIESTHOOD.

† The peace of the Lord be always with you.

 AND ALSO WITH YOU.

We shake hands or hug each other to wish God's peace to each other. Turn to page 18.

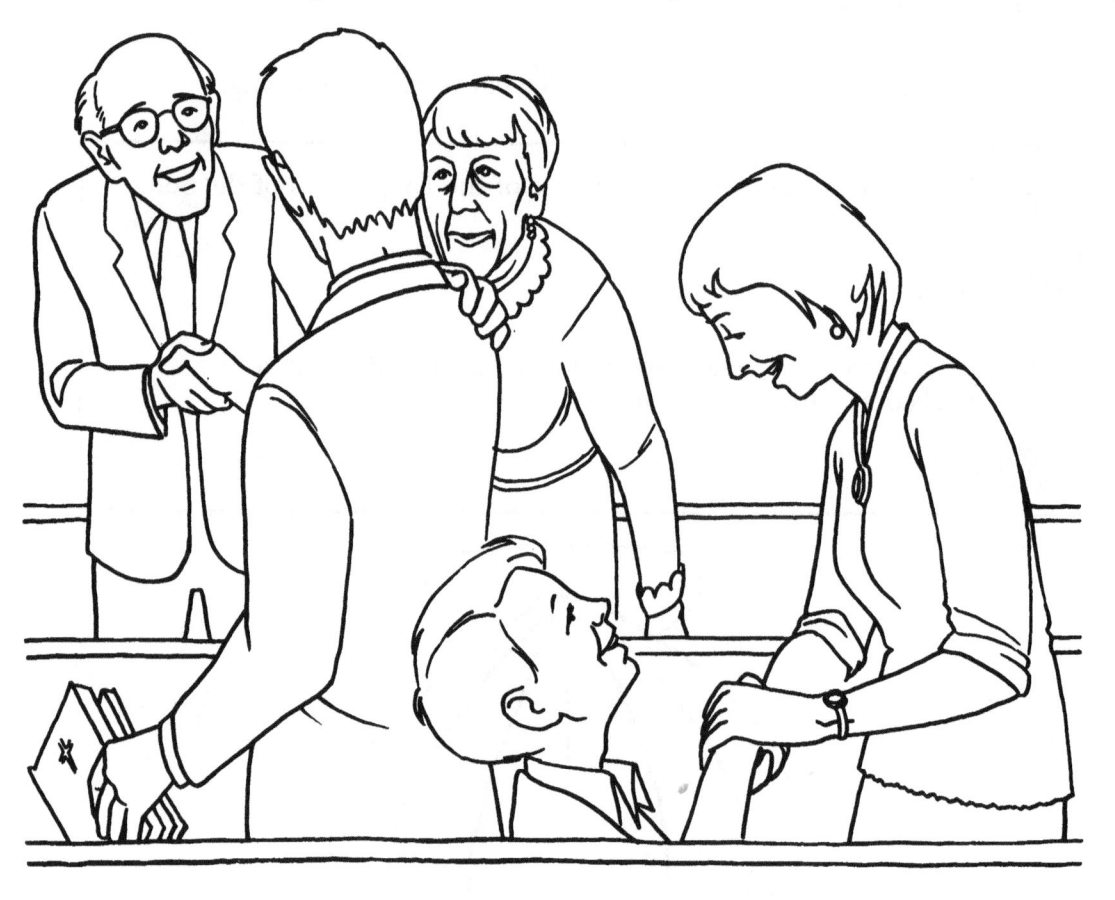

HOLY
BAPTISM

_____

PRAYERS OF THE PEOPLE  or

PRAY
FOR THE
WORLD
AND THE
CHURCH

We pray for the whole Church. We pray for our nation and our leaders. We pray for the whole world.

We pray for our neighbors and friends. We pray for people who are sick or in trouble. We pray for people who have died.

16

CONFESSION

We tell God we are sorry for things we have done wrong. We are sorry, too, for things we should have done, but didn't do. We will try harder to love God and to follow Him.

ABSOLUTION

God loves us. He will certainly forgive us.

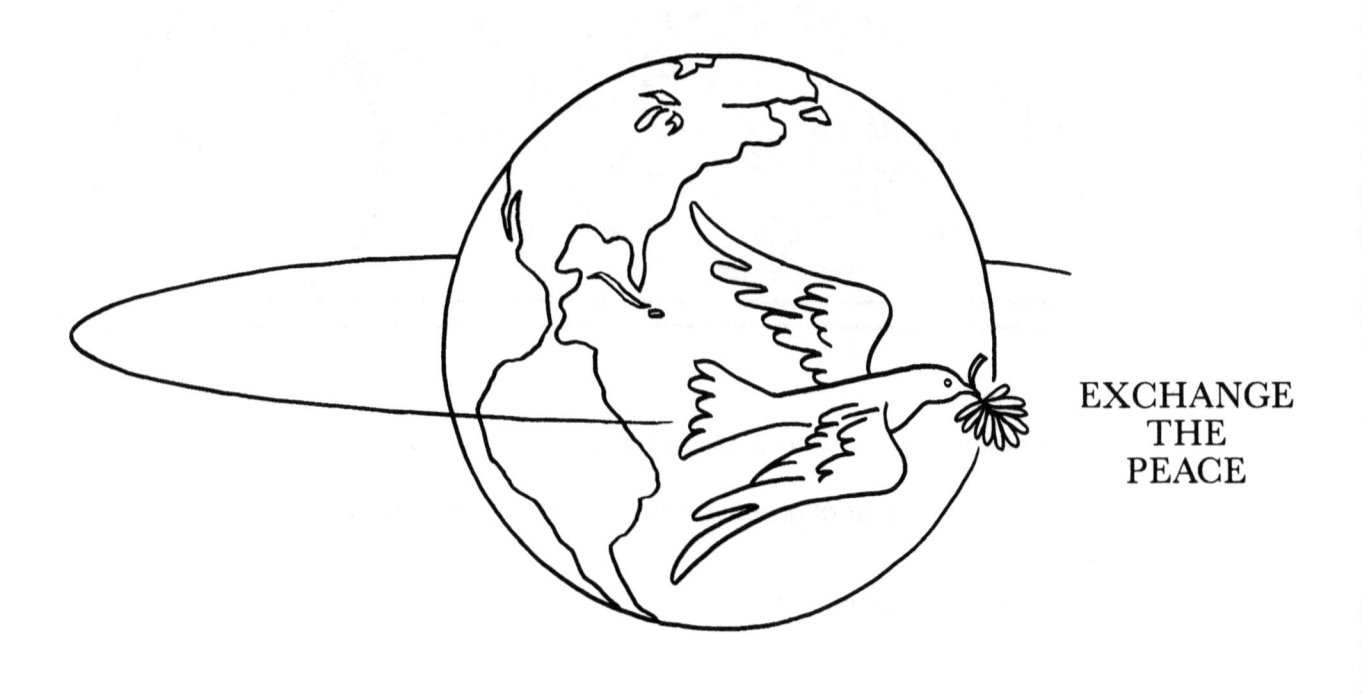

EXCHANGE
THE
PEACE

THE PEACE

✝ The peace of the Lord be always with you.

AND ALSO WITH YOU.

We shake hands or hug each other. We wish God's peace to each other.

17

OFFERTORY  or

We offer ourselves to God. We give money to the church to help us do God's work, and to thank God for all His blessings.

PREPARE THE TABLE

The priest may wash his hands as he prays.

People carry our gifts of bread and wine and our gifts of money up to the altar.

All our gifts are offered to God.

 We may sing this hymn, or some other song of thanksgiving:

> ♪ PRAISE GOD FROM WHOM ALL BLESSINGS FLOW.
> PRAISE HIM ALL CREATURES HERE BELOW.
> PRAISE HIM ABOVE YE HEAVENLY HOST.
> PRAISE FATHER, SON AND HOLY GHOST.
> AMEN.

THE GREAT THANKSGIVING

† The Lord be with you.

AND ALSO WITH YOU.

† Lift up your hearts.

WE LIFT THEM TO THE LORD.

† Let us give thanks to the Lord our God.

IT IS RIGHT TO GIVE HIM THANKS AND PRAISE.

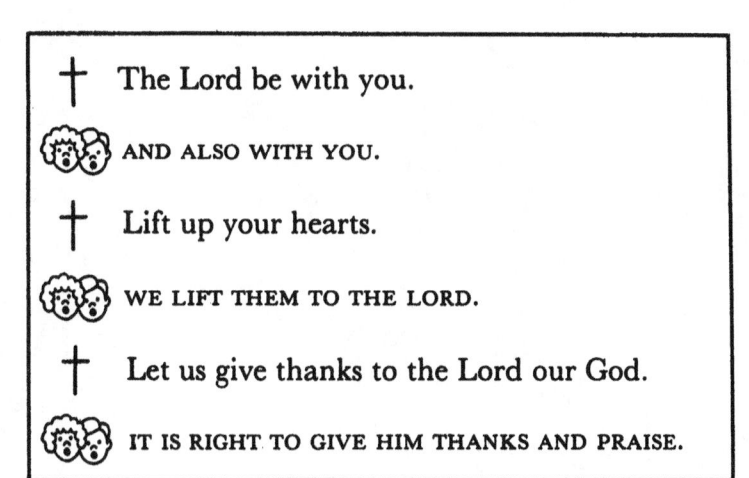

MAKE
THE
EUCHARIST

Sing or say:

♪ HOLY, HOLY, HOLY LORD,
GOD OF POWER AND MIGHT,
HEAVEN AND EARTH ARE FULL OF YOUR GLORY.
HOSANNA IN THE HIGHEST.
BLESSED IS HE WHO COMES IN THE NAME OF THE LORD.
HOSANNA IN THE HIGHEST.

THE GREAT THANKS-GIVING

At the Last Supper, the night before Jesus died, he gave us a special gift.

Jesus took bread, gave thanks for it, broke it, and gave it to his disciples.

He said, "Take, eat: This is my Body."

Then, after supper, Jesus took wine.

He gave thanks for it, and said to his disciples, "Drink this, all of you: This is my Blood. Do this for the remembrance of me."

Today we offer our bread and wine in the same way, just as Jesus told us to do.

20

THE
GREAT
THANKS-
GIVING

The special gift is Jesus himself.

He is with us in his special way in the Eucharist.

✝ Therefore we proclaim the mystery of faith:

CHRIST HAS DIED.

CHRIST IS RISEN.

CHRIST WILL COME AGAIN.

✝ By him, and with him, and in him, in the unity of the Holy
Spirit, all honor and glory is yours, Almighty Father, now and for
ever.

AMEN.

✝ And now, as our Savior Christ has taught us, we are bold to say,

OUR FATHER, WHO ART IN HEAVEN,

HALLOWED BE THY NAME,

THY KINGDOM COME,

THY WILL BE DONE,

ON EARTH AS IT IS IN HEAVEN.

GIVE US THIS DAY OUR DAILY BREAD.

AND FORGIVE US OUR TRESPASSES,

AS WE FORGIVE THOSE WHO TRESPASS AGAINST US.

AND LEAD US NOT INTO TEMPTATION,

BUT DELIVER US FROM EVIL.

FOR THINE IS THE KINGDOM, AND THE POWER, AND THE GLORY,

FOR EVER AND EVER.

AMEN.

THE BREAKING OF THE BREAD

The priest breaks the Bread we have offered.

> ✝ Christ our Passover is sacrificed for us.
>
> 🐑 THEREFORE LET US KEEP THE FEAST.
>
> ✝ The Gifts of God for the People of God. Take them in remembrance that Christ died for you, and feed on him in your hearts by faith, with thanksgiving.

The priest and people share
the Bread and Wine at the altar.

**SHARE
THE GIFTS
OF GOD**

The priest says:

> † The Body of Christ, the bread of heaven.
> The Blood of Christ, the cup of salvation.

We may answer,

> 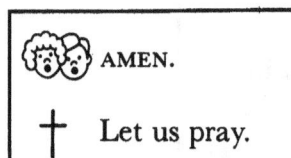 AMEN.
>
> † Let us pray.

We thank God for accepting us and feeding us. We ask God to send
us out to love Him every day. The priest may bless us.

> † Let us go forth in the name of Christ.
>
> THANKS BE TO GOD.

The celebration of the Eucharist is over for today. We pray quietly, and we ask God's help to live as Christians all week long.

RECESSIONAL

♪ Look in the Hymnal.

The priest, acolytes and choir leave the altar.

sunday   monday   tuesday   wednesday   thursday   friday   saturday

SHARE
THE GIFTS
OF GOD

1. Altar Cloth — This is a cloth that covers the altar, or table. It is also called Fair Linen.

2. Burse — This square pocket carries some of the small cloths used on the altar. The corporal and purificators are put in here. The burse is the color of the current church season, so it matches the vestments the priest wears. It is put on top of the chalice and paten when the priest is going to and from the altar.

3. Candles — These are lit at the beginning of each service and put out after the service is over.

4. Chalice — This silver or gold cup holds the wine that is consecrated at the Eucharist.

5. Ciborium — This gold or silver box has a cover, and it is used to hold the bread that is consecrated and given to the people at the Eucharist.

6. Corporal — It is a linen napkin that is spread over the altar cloth. The chalice, paten, and other communion vessels are placed on it.

7. Epistle Side — As you look at the altar from your seat, this is the right side of the altar. The Epistle is traditionally read from this side.

8. Gospel Side — As you look at the altar, this is the left side of the altar. The Gospel is usually read from this side, by custom.

9. Pall — This small, square piece of cardboard or metal is covered with linen. It is used to cover the chalice.

10. Paten — This is a round, flat gold or silver plate. The priest uses it to hold the consecrated bread during the Eucharist.

11. Purificator — After we share the bread and wine at the altar, this small linen napkin is used to wipe out the chalice.

12. Veil — This silk square covers the communion vessels when they are not being used on the altar. It is the color of the church season, too.

J

ALTAR

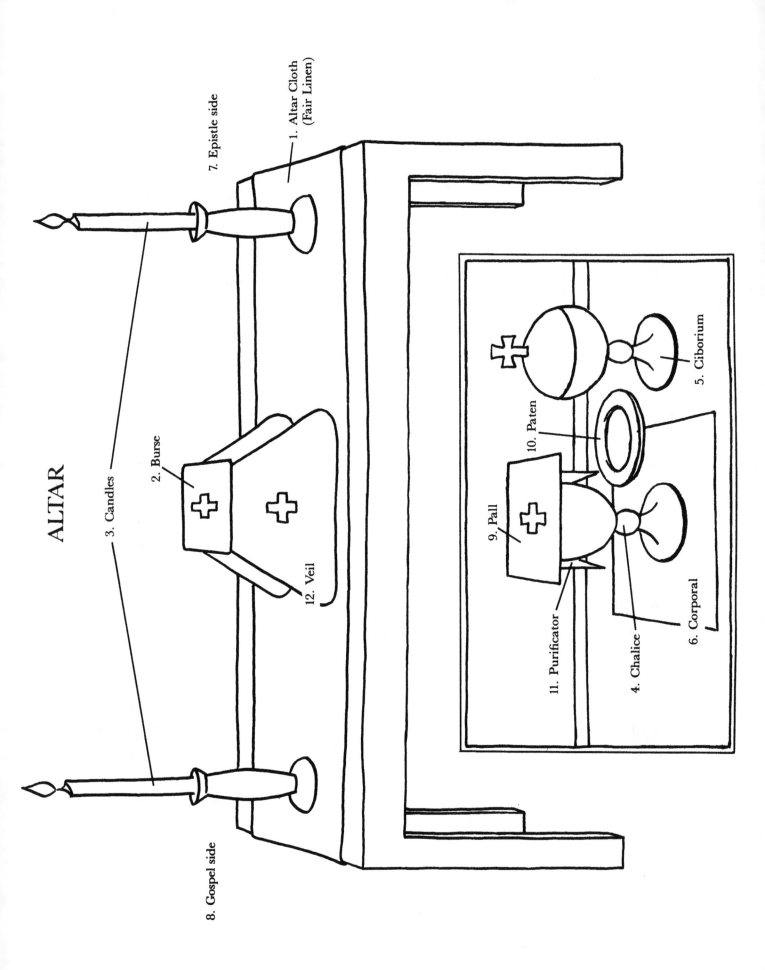

1. Altar Cloth (Fair Linen)
2. Burse
3. Candles
4. Chalice
5. Ciborium
6. Corporal
7. Epistle side
8. Gospel side
9. Pall
10. Paten
11. Purificator
12. Veil

I

PRIEST

These vestments are worn by priests when they celebrate the Eucharist. The vestments are special clothes that have been worn by priests for hundreds of years. Each article is worn for a reason.

1. Alb — This is a long, white garment that covers the priest from his shoulders to his ankles. The white color is for purity.

2. Amice — This linen collar is worn with the alb. It is white, too.

3. Chasuble — The large, oval robe with an opening in the center for the priest's head is usually the color of the current church season. It is like the robe that soldiers put on Jesus after they scourged him.

4. Cincture — This is a cloth or rope that the priest wears around his waist. It stands for the cords that tied Jesus' hands.

5. Cope — The bishop's cape is long and circular. It is also the color of the church season.

6. Crozier — This curved staff that the bishop carries is a shepherd's crook. It shows that the bishop is the leader of the flock.

7. Mitre — This is the bishop's pointed hat. The points stand for the tongues of fire that appeared over the heads of the apostles on Pentecost. The two streamers down the back are symbols of living water.

8. Stole — The long, narrow piece of silk cloth that is the color of the church season can be worn hanging straight down from the priest's neck, or it can cross over the chest. It reminds us of Jesus' burdens.

BISHOP

Bishops are priests, too. They are the head of a group of Christians in a certain place. Their vestments show that they are shepherds. The people in the churches are members of their flock.

VESTMENTS

1. Alb
2. Amice
3. Chasuble
4. Cincture
5. Cope
6. Crozier
7. Mitre
8. Stole

G

ASCENSION

WHITE
for joy

Ascension Thursday occurs on the fortieth day from Easter. It recalls Jesus' leaving his earthly home. The season lasts just ten days, till Pentecost Sunday.

PENTECOST SUNDAY

RED
for tongues
of fire

This Sunday celebrates the Holy Spirit's coming to strengthen and enlighten the disciples. It is the fiftieth day from Easter.

PENTECOST

GREEN
for hope
and growth

This is the longest season of the church year, lasting until Advent. We celebrate the growth of the church, the spread of the good news, and we study about Jesus' life.

F

CELEBRATION COLORS

SEASONS

SYMBOLS

LENT

Lent begins on Ash Wednesday and continues for forty days. During this time we think about Jesus' fasting, sacrifice, and death.

PURPLE
for sorrow
and kingship

HOLY WEEK

This is a part of Lent that comes between Palm Sunday and Easter. We celebrate Jesus' triumphant arrival in Jerusalem on Palm Sunday, and the events which led to his death and burial.

WHITE
for joy
RED
for blood

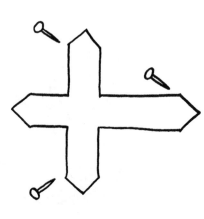

EASTER

This season celebrates Jesus Christ's victory over death. He is risen!

WHITE
for joy
and triumph

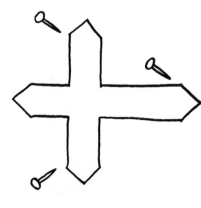

E

CELEBRATION COLORS	SEASONS	SYMBOLS

SEASONS

ADVENT

This is the first season of the church year. It lasts for four Sundays before Christmas Day. During Advent we get ready for Jesus' birth.

PURPLE
for kingship

CHRISTMAS

This season begins on December 25 and lasts until January 6. We celebrate the birth of our Savior, Jesus Christ.

WHITE
for joy

EPIPHANY

Epiphany begins on the day set aside to recall the visit of the three wise men to Bethlehem. This season goes from January 6 to Ash Wednesday.

GREEN
for hope

continued on next page

D